Streams of GOLD

Streams of
GOLD

Joyce Southern Bennett

To order additional copies of this book, contact:
Xlibris Corporation
1-888-795-4274
www.Xlibris.com
Orders@Xlibris.com
118817

CONTENTS

Embracing Today 9

The Truth And Life 11

He's Still The Shepherd 13

His Light..15

I Feel Home 17

The Dayspring 19

Anchor Of Ages...21

Old New Eyes 23

Be Still And Know 26

God's Child...29

It Took The Blood 32

A Make Believe Letter 35

The Shepherd Is Here...41

Don't Let My Song Die In Me...43

I Know Where You Are 45

He Knows Every Trail From My Valley......................................51

Move Up The Mountain 57

I Love You, My Jesus 59

There's Cool Water In The Valley 62

My Guest Of Honor 64

I Want To Hit Golden Streets Running 67

Come ON Sundown 70

God Allowed Nails To Fix Everything.......................................73

Let's Go To The Other Side 77

Vitory At Daylight 86

Arrayed In White 91

Paper Doll Years 95

He'll Be Coming Through The Clouds 100

Winds Of Revival...108

INTRODUCTION

At times, in my lifetime, I have had a hunger to write. When I was a teenager, I would sit on the porch at the house (it wasn't that old then) and write poems. I Have been writing songs for years. I have enclosed a lot of them with my Morning Writing.

My little sister, Barbara, and I, use to sit on the porch banister and sing. We even, Use to perform on old saw dust piles. Our cousin, Ellen, use to climb up the saw dust Pile and perform with us.

I really didn't think I could write a Devotional Book, but felt, I was suppose to try. The inspiration came from someone higher than me. He gives me Strength, Hope and Joy. When the presence of the Lord, closes in, I feel as if, I could still climb, a Saw Dust pile.

EMBRACING TODAY

Jesus tells us in (John 14:1) "Let not your heart be troubled: Ye believe in God, Believe also in me." JOHN 16:24, "Hitherto have ye asked nothing in my name: ask, and ye shall receive, that your joy may be full."

I had a doctor's appointment yesterday for a regular checkup. I had pondered on asking my doctor to send me to an Orthopedic. A pinched nerve was giving me fits, from my lower back, going down my right leg.

A still small voice spoke to my spirit and said, "Do you remember me telling you to run the night you went to a revival meeting at Brother Chris's church?"

"Yes, Lord, I remember," I answered.

"Do you remember, me telling you, I would take care of your back, if you would run?"

I remembered how awesome the spirit was, when I ran that night. I felt, as if, I was wrapped in a warm blanket.

"Lord," I said, "There's no need in me going any where else. You promised to heal me."

The Bible tells us in the last part of 1 Samuel: 15:22, "Behold to obey is better than sacrifice, and to harken than the fat of rams."

I look across the small stream from where I sit on the backporch. The stream divides the two yards from the old house, where I was raised and where I now live.

The old house has been a place of tranquility for me over the years. I've been able to see it from my kitchen window, as well, as the backporch. It is snaky now and is rotting down, with bushes and brambles closing in around it.

The laughter no longer echoes from the past. Skinned knees from playing are almost forgotten, a brother, bravely, joining the Marine Corp., little sister growing up, the excitement when the two older sisters would visit. Daddy died, while him and Momma were still in the house.

Time passes, memories fade, but how precious is life to embrace memories we have and still be able to embrace each day we have.

His Voice

I'm so thankful, I know, my Savior,
He promised, He'll never depart.
When He saved my soul and forgave me,
Then His freedom released my heart.

CHORUS:
Now, I listen for harps in the distance,
Riding on the wings of the wind.
I listen for heavenly music,
And the voice of Jesus, my friend.

Oh, at times, I've walked with sorrow,
I've asked, my Jesus, when will it end?
Then the music echo's from the distance,
And I hear the voice of my friend.
I watch the sun, way up the mountain,
It shines in streams of pure gold.
I just stand in awe and I listen,
To a voice that will never grow old.

Joyce Bennett

THE TRUTH AND LIFE

JOHN 14: 6, "Jesus saith unto him (talking to Thomas) I am the way, the truth, and the life: No man cometh unto the Father but by me."

I was amazed to see the beautiful sunset, last evening, when I closed the front door. I went immediately, to the backporch, where I could have a grand view of it going down.

By the time I walked to the backporch, the sun had already turned into a blazing bonfire of yellow, orange and gold. I watched it, in all it's glory, as it slowly diminished over the distant ridge.

I stood awhile, feeling the silence of the twilight and the peace of God overshadowing me. PHILIPPIANS 4: 7, "And the peace of God, which passeth all understanding shall keep your hearts and minds through Christ Jesus.

I longed to stay outside, even as darkness claimed the earth but, common sense led me back inside.

There is so much of God's beauty, I look upon, but fail to see. Time and circum-stances seem to have a way of blocking one's view. I'm reminded of part of First Corinthians 13:12, "For now we see through a glass darkly:" Praise the Lord, if we continue to follow Him, one day we will see Him face to face. He truly is, the way, the truth, and life.

Jesus Is The Truth And Life

CHORUS:
Jesus is the way the truth and life,
Christ Jesus, is the way for me.
He listens when I pray, My sins are rolled away,
I once was bound, but now I'm free.

I no longer live in depths of dark valleys,
God sent spiritual wings to higher ground.
His truth unfolds to the light of His coming,
I have a new life, no longer bound.

I can look past all clouds of self-will,
And let my Savior's light shine through me.
I will come out from storm winds of doubt,
He's the truth and life eternally.

Joyce Bennett

HE'S STILL THE SHEPHERD

PSALM 37:25, "I have been young, and now am old, yet have I not seen the righteous forsaken, nor his seed begging bread."

My daughter, Sue, and granddaughter, Rebekah, and me, decided to make a small trip to the next town to buy groceries, due to the supermarket there having cheaper prices than the ones in our town.

We were amazed at the majestic, fog-covered mountains, we could see from the high-way. ISAIAH 54: 10, "For the mountains shall depart, and the hills be removed; but my kindness shall not depart from thee, neither shall the covenant of my peace be removed, saith the Lord that hath mercy on thee."

Rain had set in, steady, but not a downpour. We couldn't see where the mountains ended and the sky began. PSALM 144: 5, "Bow thy heavens, O Lord, and come down: touch the mountains, and they shall smoke."

We are so blessed to live where God's handi-work is strewn in any direction we choose to go.

After buying groceries and getting back to familiar territory, Sue noticed the river was rising, as we passed the river close to home. The ripple had changed to a steady flow. Rocks were hidden on the bottom of the riverbed, that had been so visible during the recent drought. The water splashed more forcefully against the uncovered rocks, spraying higher the cold mist and foam.

PRAISE THE LORD! HE is the one who sends the rain upon the earth, to the rivers, streams, wells, and springs. MATTHEW 5:45, "That ye may be the children of your Father which is in heaven: for He maketh his sun to rise on the evil and on the good, and sendeth rain on the just and on the unjust."

He's Still The Shepherd

(Of The Hills)

I will lift my eyes to higher places,
And forget this world and it's frills.
I'll seek a heavenly mist, through life's busy-ness,
For, He's still the Shepherd of the hills.

CHORUS:
God's still the Shepherd of the hills,
He's still the Shepherd of the hills.
He made the mountains, valleys, and the fields,
And He's still the Shepherd of the hills.

Time gets a way and swiftly changes,
Sometimes, I forget to seek His will.
But, it's like a fresh rain, when I call on His name,
For, He's still the Shepherd of the hills.

He leads me through the briars and trenches,
Heavenly places give my soul a thrill,
I will follow Him onward, and keep pressing homeward,
For, He's still the Shepherd of the hills.

Joyce Bennett

HIS LIGHT

JOHN 8:12, Jesus tells us, "I am the light of the world: he that followeth me shall not walk in darkness, but shall have the light of life."

Some men from the electric company in our area, cut some trees under the electric wires in my backyard. I didn't like the trees being cut, due to the clearing making a clearer view of my mother's empty mobile home. Momma moved into the single wide a short time after daddy died.

Even though, it is cool and a fine mist is falling, I had a hurried cup of coffee on the backporch. I noticed, my eyes kept going past momma's place to the neighbor's house next door. The house was brightly lit, like a city on the hill.

PRAISE THE LORD; I was able to look past my circumstances to the light. Light seems to always make a difference. The worst rock pile seems to look different when God's morning sunlight shines upon it.

At this writing, my husband, Bill, went on to be with the Lord, three years ago. My mother went on two years ago, and we lost my sister, Geneva, five months ago. I know their all with Jesus, where there is no more pain or suffering. REVELATION21:4 tells us, "God shall wipe away all tears from their eyes; and there shall be no more death, neither sorrow, nor crying, neither shall there be no more pain: for the former things are passed away."

His Light

Oh, the hillside here looks like winter,
The leaves have all blown a-way.
But, I'm headed a way past the sunset,
Where the light will shine there all day.

CHORUS:
His joy will ease all sorrow,
The fall will turn into spring.
The dead in Christ, will rise tomorrow,
I'll see loved ones and Jesus, my king.

Many people still walk in darkness,
They forget redemption has come.
His light will shine through the shadows,
As we praise Him, when the day is done.

Oh, we won't need a candle in heaven,
For, there will never come no night,
When the sun goes down there forever,
For, Jesus Christ, Himself is the light.

Joyce Bennett

I FEEL HOME

PSALM 118:24, "This is the day which the Lord hath made; we will rejoice and be glad in it."

I felt a special feeling in my home this morning. It was a feeling, I hadn't felt since Childhood, living in the old house. It's a special calmness, a tranquil silence, it's as if, You know your family is near, but you can not see them. Their warmth and presence Surrounds you.

HEBREWS 12:1, "Wherefore seeing we also are compassed about with so great a Cloud of witnesses; let us lay aside every weight, and the sin which doth so easily beset us, and let us run with patience the race that is set before us." I look beyond the yard to the lush green bushes. The trees are beginning to bud and White dogwood blooms are beginning to dot the hillside. Spring has come, bringing With it, brisk, refreshing air.

People, like greenery breaking forth, also, need rest. I remember, when I was a child, We didn't do much in the winter months. We did, "The Things," as we called them. The Children went to school. Barbara, my little sister, and me helped carry in firewood and Water. Our brother, Bevis, helped saw wood and helped daddy feed what farm animals We had. Momma cooked a lot on the wood heater in the front room. She was always a Frugal person and the heater already had a good fire burning, due to the cold weather.

I'm reminded of this scripture. It's not a favorite of mine, but it is true. ECCLESIATES: 1:4, "One generation passeth away, and another generation cometh: But the earth abideth for ever."

It is time for me to regroup. My heart wants to cling to a portion back there, but His Unseen hand is reaching down and leading me forward.

I can almost see Bill, sitting in his power chair, looking across the way, as if, he's in A deep study. A cool breeze whispers against my face. I swing gently in the swing and Begin to commune higher.

I Feel Home Settling In

CHORUS:
I feel home settling in,
I've been wondering, way too long.
This old world is rapid fading,
I see a bright light, I'm going home.

This old house is growing dimmer,
I've given away, nearly all I own.
The sun is setting on my journey,
Oh, take my wrap, I'm going home.

I hear a trumpet in the distance,
Heaven's bells keep ringing on.
Pearly gates are swinging open,
On wings of love, I'm going home.

I feel my Savior, drawing closer,
I hear loud praise around His throne.
The angels sing and loved ones beckon,
I'll say good-by now, I'm going home.

Joyce Bennett

THE DAYSPRING

ISAIAH 66:12, "For thus saith the Lord, I will extend peace to her like a river, and the glory of the Gentiles like a flowing stream."

The brisk, fresh air along with birds flying and calling to one another, greeted me This morning. A patchy fog clings between trees, bringing the morning, even more Peace. PSALM 72:3, "The mountains shall bring forth peace to the people, and the little Hills by righteousness."

Where I live, certainly isn't the Great Smoky Mountains, but this is my haven of Rest. I am so blessed to be able to sit quietly each morning and see God's beauty all Around me. He seeks our quiet times and I seek Him early.

LUKE 1:78, "Through the tender mercies of our God; whereby the dayspring from on high hath visited us."

The Dayspring

Oh, I have read of Nether Springs, they are lower than the rest,
I'm reminded of deep joy, that comes from a test.
I know a dayspring, who came from on high,
It's where I go, when I'm thirsty and dry.

CHORUS:
He's the dayspring from heaven, He's sent from on high,
He saves the vilest sinner and hears the heart's cry.
He's Jesus, my Lord, on whom I rely,
And He still waits on the thirsty and dry.

Oh, there's a place down in the ocean, where no man has ever been,
And there's a deep love, that gives peace within.
It reaches the lowest depths, goes higher than the sky,
It's where I go, when I'm thirsty and dry.

I have read about a river, flowing from the throne of God,
The water is clear as crystal, and on the banks the angels trod.
I'm going to see the dayspring, nevermore to say good-by,
And up there, no soul will be thirsty and dry.

Joyce Bennett

ANCHOR OF AGES

MATTHEW13: 44, "Again, the kingdom of heaven is like unto treasure hid in a field; the which when a man hath found, he hideth, and for joy thereof goeth and selleth all that he hath, and buyeth that field."

I noticed yesterday, when I took a walk, three black rocks, almost uncovered, from A hard rain. I removed the mud and picked up all of them. Two of the rocks were Shaped almost, like arrow heads. The other one was old, but not unusual.

The rocks brought back old memories. Momma had our report cards, and two or three Black arrow heads, and one old penny, in an old Blair box.

Bevis was into swapping Comic Books at school. It was the greatest delight to find, A Porky Pig or a Bugs Bunny, I hadn't read. PSALM 37:4, tells us to, "Delight thyself also in the Lord; and he shall give thee the desires of thine heart." For a twelve-year-old Girl then, there was no greater delight, than to get your hands on a Looney Tunes Comic Book.

One night we were sitting around the wood heater. We probably were all reading, Except Barbara. She was too young to read much, when Daddy commented, "Our Family sure is content, for us to be as broke as we are."

"We got money," all of us children declared. "We got the Oliver Penny."

We could speak with authority. We knew we had money. If we have, Jesus Christ, In our lives, we can profess with authority, "I know, Jesus Christ."

LUKE 9:1, "Then he called his disciples together, and gave them power and authority over all devils, and to cure diseases."

Anchor Of Ages

When earthly cares surround me, through this world's dark smog,
May my faith in my Savior, see clear through the fog.
For, He's my harbor of safety, Master of my sea,
The anchor of ages and best friend to me.

CHORUS:
I have cast my hook and all my life-line,
To the anchor of ages, where my soul is entwined.
He's unmovable, unchangeable, solid, I see,
The anchor of ages and best friend, to me.

He's in the secret place of thunder, holds lightning in His hands,
He can ride on the wind and make oceans dry land,
Yet, He gave His life freely, so I could go free,
The anchor of ages and best friend to me.

Joyce Bennett

OLD NEW EYES

PSALM 19:1, "The heavens declare the glory of God; and the firmament sheweth His handi-work."

The beautiful green leaves, from the surrounding trees are blocking my view, this Morning of the old house and momma's trailer, leaving a beautiful spot in between, Looking like a majestic hollow. Isn't that just like, Jesus, giving me my own hollow? The early sun seems to be streaming down, instead of merely beaming or shining.

JOHN 14:27, "Peace I leave with you, my peace I give unto you; not as the world giveth, give I unto you. Let not your heart be troubled, neither let it be afraid."

I think about some people, who have to look out their windows or across porches at Shabby houses or bleak ugly walls. I am so blessed to look across my backyard to a Beautiful place, my Lord, has created, just for me.

A friend of mine, Sister Dottie, a minister, prophesied to me. She said, I would Be standing at the kitchen sink, and I would begin to shout in the Holy Spirit.

Yesterday afternoon, I was washing dishes at the sink and sure enough, I heard a small Still voice begin to speak to my heart and say, "I'm standing between you and Bill." I began to shout. Praise the Lord! Bill was just on the other side of Jesus.

The Lord, also gave me a vision of a little girl skipping down the path from the Cemetery, at the church where Bill and Rex, my son are buried. I can remember the little girl wore a jumper with a ruffled blouse and wore black patent shoes. I don't know how I knew it, but I knew my joy had returned.

JEREMIAH 33:3, "Call unto me, and I will answer thee, and shew thee great and Mighty things, which thou knowest not."

Bill had such beautiful blue eyes.

Old New Eyes

We were in our thirties when we met,
As long as I have my mind, I won't forget.
You were a macho man; your temper could arise,
You look at me, now differently, with old new eyes.

CHORUS:
Old new eyes, old new eyes,
You look at me so sweetly, with old new eyes.
How much you really love me, you now realize,
It shows so deeply in those old new eyes.

You liked your own way and I did too,
We grew close together, like many will do.
We had thirty years, how the time flies,
You look at me so precious, with old new eyes.

Sickness has brought dark days to both of us,
But, through it all, we also, found a lot of trust.
Our hands cling together and my heart cries,
As you look at me, my darling, with old new eyes.

Joyce Bennett

William T. Bennett
"Bill"

BE STILL AND KNOW

EXODUS 15:26, God told Moses and the children of Israel, "If thou wilt diligently harken to the voice of the Lord, thy God, and wilt do that which is right in His sight, I will put none of these diseases upon thee, which I have brought upon the Egyptians: (meaning Pharaoh and his army) for I am the Lord that healeth thee."

Sometimes, at church, when the Holy Spirit is moving, and saints begin to rejoice, I Feel, as if, I could run up a mountain, down it, and back around it. I think of this, when I Take a short walk, then huff and puff, before I make it back to the yard.

I ponder on my situation, and realize, when the Holy Ghost takes over, we are not in Our own strength. We take on His strength when this happens.

Bill, and our youngest son, Lee, and I lived a few years in Florida. I remember, at one Of the churches, we attended, seeing a lady jump and shout on one leg. When the spirit Was moving, she would jump from her seat and dance a jig on one foot. I asked the Lord Then, "Lord, Please give me a portion of what that lady has."

The Lord didn't give me a portion of what that saint had; He gave me my own portion. When the spirit is moving, even here at home, when I'm having my devotion, I feel like Walking and praising the Lord. I know, we are not all alike, some cry, some have goose Bumps while some sit quietly and enjoys the presence of the Lord. I don't believe it Matters how we worship as long as we have Salvation and obey Him.

The Lord gave me some songs, several years ago, while I helped Bill pick up dead Chickens. A neighbor hired Bill, to pick up the chickens a couple hours each morning. He wasn't able to do this alone. I was working in the evenings in a store and had time To go with him and help. The Lord would give me songs while we worked. I would Write them down when we returned home.

PSALM 46:10, Be still, and know that I am God: I will be exalted among the heathen, I will be exalted in the earth."

Be Still, My Child And Know

CHORUS:
Be still, my child and know, I'm with you where you go,
I was in the driest desert, where the flowers wouldn't grow.
I was in the darkest valley, where you were praying so,
I'm here today, be still, my child and know.

I was there at the crossroads, when you cried out to me,
Your soul was in bondage, there, I set you free.
I gave you peace, and gave you joy, these things, I did bestow,
Trust me completely, be still, my child, and know.

I'm there in the morning mist, I see storms come and go,
I'm aware of every trial, each heartache below.
Remember the old paths, set your eyes on heaven's glow,
Keep leaning on me, be still, my child, and know.

Joyce Bennett

This is another chicken house song.

I Didn't Find My Answer
On The Mountaintop

My road sometimes is rocky and briars are in the way,
When I can't find my way across, I just stop and pray.
My lord makes my path straight, all in His time,
I didn't find my answer on the mountaintop; I found it in the climb.

CHORUS:
I found it in the climb; I found it in the climb,
I didn't find my answer on the mountaintop; I found it in the climb.
I kept on climbing, knowing there was more to find,
I didn't find my answer on the mountaintop; I found it in the climb.

Life's winds would blow, oh, so mighty hard,
And this old feeble body would get so weak and tired.
But, I kept pressing forward, forgetting those things behind,
For, I didn't find my answer on the mountaintop; He was here—in my climb.

Joyce Bennett

GOD'S CHILD

Psalm 46:1-2, "God is our refuge and strength, a very present help in trouble." (2) "Therefore will not we fear, though the earth be removed, and though the mountains be Carried into the midst of the sea."

It was always a treat to go with Bill, to the woods to haul firewood. The last time we Went; it was an, altogether, different experience.

I was still working in the evenings, but had time to go with Bill, one morning, to bring In a load of wood.

Someone, Bill knew, had sawed down several trees and told, Bill to go and get all the Wood we needed.

When we arrived, where we had been instructed to go, we found a closed gate and a Creek to drive through.

I managed to open the gate, then Bill, drove into the creek, on to the other side. I Closed the gate and waded the shallow creek, then joined Bill back in the truck.

Bill's nerves were on edge. I could feel his nervousness. The feeling overshadowed The quiet and early morning stillness. I was hardly aware, when the sun broke out over The treetops. I didn't notice the sun filtering through the leaves and branches showing Patches of sparkling dew. I didn't notice the dampness that came with early morning. I could only feel the awful feeling, Bill was feeling.

Bill sawed the wood and we managed to fill the truck with sticks we were able to lift, Then came back to the creek and gate.

The gate fastener would not budge. Bill was in the truck, the truck was in the creek, And Bill's nerves hadn't gotten any better. The fastener was jammed and would not Move. After a while, I begin to feel a presence behind me. I thought it was the land-Owner. I waited for him to say something, but no one said a word. I turned around to See who was standing behind me. There was no one there. I tried the gate again. It Opened easily, without any trouble.

PSALM 91:11, "For He shall give His angels charge over thee, to keep thee in all thy ways."

Bill was a diabetic. I don't know, if this was why he was nervous, but I do know, The Lord had His hand on both of us. Bill, took sick later and was patient, most of the Time, throughout his illness.

God's Child

There is no situation, the Lord cannot mend,
Do you trust Him today, as your friend?
The shadow of His wings, is where to hide,
His hands are upon you, God's child.

CHORUS:
God's hands are upon you, God's child,
His hands are upon you, God's child.
He paves the way and walks by your side,
Yes, His hands are upon you, God's child.

When you are in trouble on life's stormy sea,
The Lord rides the wind, to set you free.
He's the lighthouse to safety from the raging tide,
His hands are upon you, God's child.

Joyce Bennett

IT TOOK THE BLOOD

PSALM: 9-1-2-, I will praise thee, O Lord, with my whole heart; I will shew forth all thy marvelous works." (2) "I will be glad and rejoice in thee; I will sing Praise to thy name, O thou most High."

Blackberry briars, bending with white blooms, lace the back of the yard this Morning. The sun has come up, but is still holding back the heat for the day.

I can see a small portion of the garden spot, but now is grown up in weeds. I can also, see the edge of where, I once had a bean patch.

Daddy and mamma had a large bean patch, the summer, I turned fourteen. They Planted the beans for market. I had my own six rows on the branch bank. My beans Were to help me buy some things for school. Some of my friends had nylon dresses. I wanted a nylon dress, a zipper notebook, and a new pocketbook.

My sister, Virginia, asked me, one Sunday, to go home with her, and invited me To a Revival meeting that was to last all week. I spent the week with Virginia, her Husband, Clifford, and their young son, Teddy.

I can't remember, how many young people went to the front of the church and Knelt by the old mourner's bench. I went every night, from Sunday night until Thursday Night.

Some of the saints that prayed for us would ask, "Will you give everything for, Jesus?" Well, sometime that week, I gave up Daddy and Momma, my sisters, Geneva, and Virginia, my one brother, Bevis, and even my little sister, Barbara. When the saints Would ask, "Have you given up everything." I wanted to reply, "You already have Everything I have, now leave my bean patch alone."

Thursday night, something happened, it was, as if, I had been somewhere. When I Came to reality, I was sitting on the bench, laughing.

"Why doesn't she stand?" I heard someone say. I didn't know I was suppose to Stand, but I did.

Everyone standing around me hugged me. I had salvation. My soul was Gloriously saved. PRAISE THE LORD!

Daddy and a neighbor hauled the beans to the Farmers Market in Atlanta.

Momma and Virginia, made me a beautiful blue dress, cut from a piece of nylon Cloth. I had a red drawstring pocketbook that looked like a jug. And a zipper note-Book.

Praise the Lord; He didn't want my bean patch. He only wanted me. Salvation is Free. Jesus died for us on an old rugged cross so we could have it. All He wants from Us, is obedience and trust. Salvation is a spark down in our souls that stays with us Through life, And through death.

EPHESIANS: 2-10, "For we are His workmanship, created in Christ Jesus unto good Works, which God hath before ordained that we should walk in them."

It Took The Blood

God gave Moses, a table of commandments,
There on clouded Mount Si-ni-i.
It looked like fire, the people said below,
From the cloud on the mountain so high.

CHORUS:
It took the commandments cut in stone,
But, the stone alone wouldn't do.
It took God's son, dying on Calvary,
For it took the blood of Jesus too.

The commandments made it through the water,
They have never, ever been lost.
But, it took the precious blood of Jesus,
When He bled and died on the cross.

I thank God for the commandments,
They are still in His word today,
But, it took the pure blood of Jesus,
To cleanse and wash my sins away.

Joyce Bennett

A MAKE BELIEVE LETTER

JOHN: 3-16, "For God so loved the world, that He gave His only son that Whosoever believeth in Him should not perish, but have everlasting life."

A few days ago, I heard an old hymn in my spirit. I immediately recognized the melody of one of my son, Rex's, favorite songs. Rex was fifteen, when he Went to be with the Lord. I thought a moment, then realized, it was that time of the year. The year was 1973. It has been so many years, my mind hadn't thought about the time, but my heart had.

ISAIAH: 49-15-16, "Can a woman forget her sucking child, that she should not have compassion on the son of her womb? Yea, they may forget, yet will I not forget thee." (16) "Behold I have graven thee upon the palms of my hands; thy walls are continually before me."

I was seventeen when Rex was born. I would sit him on my jewelry box, upon the Dresser and hold him. I would look at him in the mirror and remind myself that he was A little human, not a doll.

Even now, as I try to pen my thoughts to paper, it still pulls on my heart strings.

One of my favorite memories was our game, "Tater." I would place my hands on Rex's shoulders and say "Look at my big ole tater. I'm going to put it in the basement for Sunday dinner." Rex would sit down while I clicked an imaginary lock to the Basement door. I would sit down to read, and then He would jump up and run. I would Holler, "Tater," and chase him. His blue eyes would dance when I caught him. He probably was two at the time.

Rex and I always went shopping before school would start. Christmas, to me, was mostly buying Rex a little something. We never celebrated much. I believe Christmas is celebrated a little different now, than it was then.

Rex's daddy was a pouter. He would pout for days. Most of the time, we didn't know what he was pouting about.

One day, Rex was supposed to have fed his daddy's dogs. Rex had turned fifteen in January. He forget to feed the dogs. J.M., his daddy, took off his cap and slapped Rex in the face. He slapped one side of his face, then the other. I remember, it broke Rex's heart. I tried to tell him, that his daddy wasn't saved, and we needed to pray for him. In about two weeks, Rex had left home.

He caught a ride with a trucker to Gladewater, Texas. He wrote us a letter and called Me one day at work. The next call, we received, was from the sheriff, in Gladewater. He told me, there had been a confirmed drowning.

I made it, one day at a time, for awhile. I couldn't cry at home, because J.M. would Start to groan. I cried at work and at church.

It was about a year later, when I bought two dresses to wear to church. J.M. was Mad about the dresses. He went to the bank and had my name taken off our checking Account. One morning, at breakfast, I handed him a check to sign. He said, "Oh, you Know me now, when you want something."

The check was a payment on Rex's funeral bill. There is an old saying, that says, "That was the straw that broke the camel's back." I suppose, Rex, had been the reason, I had stayed, and now, he was the reason I left.

J.M. didn't show up for our divorce.

I moved to Marietta and stayed with my, Aunt Willow and Uncle Price Weaver.

They treated me like I was one of their on children. I found a job, and met Bill through His daughter, Brenda.

Bill and I married, and lived a few years in Florida, then moved back here by the Home place.

Helen, my friend and neighbor, on the hill, came home from church, one night, and saw J.M. coming out of the woods near our home. J.M., would wait part of the time down at the fork in the road, not far from our home.

The problem with J.M., was always in the back of my mind, but it worried Bill and Momma, more than it did me. J.M., parked his truck about two miles from us, and lived in his truck, until the Authorities made him move.

We only had a truck. Bill didn't like being home, without a way to go. We still didn't know the motive behind, J.M., moving near us. Bill would always take me to work and come back after me. I heard, sometime, during the last year I worked, that J.M. had died.

I believe, Rex, was taken from the evil to come. Some years later, Rex's first Cousin and best friend, Bucky, had an accident. A tree fell on Bucky. He lived two weeks after the accident. The Lord gave me the same scripture for Bucky.

ISAIAH: 57-1, "The righteous perisheth, and no man layeth it to heart, and Merciful men are taken away, none considering that the righteous is taken away, from the evil to come."

I hope we all Fly Away, on some Uncloudy Day, to go be with, Jesus Christ, the Rock of Ages, and by His Amazing Grace, surely we will Understand it Better By and By.

A Make Believe Letter

A few months ago, we received a letter,
It was from our only son.
He had always wanted to be a cowboy,
And the urge for roaming won.
The letter seemed so happy,
As he wrote about a rodeo.
He spoke of calf roping, and to bed he had to go.
How happy we were to hear,
From our loved one, so dear
To know and to feel, he was all right.
But, sitting here, this thought came to me tonight.

Oh, the happy letter, that he would write now,
Life compared to there, wasn't much anyhow.
That big horse ranch, he had dreamed about.
Nobody here, had much time, and seemed worn out.
Don't you know, it would say,
I've had a fine day.
I've rode horses and had such a wonderful time.
And what's so good, they seem to be mine.
There's no rules, no need for any.
And every where you look, there's always plenty.
I have new jeans, and a new jacket,

I don't ever get cold,
I have a new guitar, with strings of pure gold.
I have a new cowboy hat,
And the things, I wanted, don't worry about that.
Give my clothes to someone who needs them because I'm all right,
I know you and Daddy loved me, with all your might.
But, nobody's love can match, the love of Jesus, you see,
And He loved a teenager like me.
I went in swimming and went out too deep,
In Jesus' arms, I fell asleep.

A barefooted little boy, just like he came,
Jimmy Rex, was his name.
He loved and was loved,
Yet, he knew hardships too,
But, we know that's life as we pass through.
The path is lonely now, but Jesus, is the way,
We'll press on and trust the Lord,
And wait for that great Reunion day.

Joyce (Dockery) at the time.
September, 1973

L-R   Eddy   Sharon   Rex
        (Bucky)   (Bucky's sister)

THE SHEPHERD IS HERE

EXODUS 33: 21-22, The Lord was speaking to Moses, And He said, "Behold There is a place by me, and thou shalt stand upon a rock; (22) and it shall come to pass, While my glory passeth by, that I will put thee in a cleft of the rock, and will cover thee With my hand while I pass by."

I didn't go to the back porch this morning. The spirit of the Lord, filled my living-room, while I had my devotion. I am so honored to have a personal relationship with My Lord and Savior, Jesus Christ.

I think of the priest of old, when the Holy Ghost filled the temple. ISAIAH 6:1, "In the year that King Uzziah died, I saw also the Lord sitting upon a throne, high and lifted up.

The Shepherd truly has been here this morning.

The Shepherd Is Here

CHORUS:
The Shepherd is here—The Shepherd is here,
He is here—He is here—He is here.
Give Him your troubles and your cares,
Give Him your worries and your fears,
He is here—He is here—He is here.

Where are the lost sheep wandering in dry pastures?
The Shepherd is waiting, by waters cool and still.
He wants to gather His little ones to Him,
Come from the valley to His perfect will.

Come to the Shepherd's healing streams of water,
He stands waiting and reaches out to you,
Oh, won't you let Him, lead you up higher?
His spirit is falling, like the morning dew.

Joyce Bennett

DON'T LET MY SONG DIE IN ME

JOHN 10:10, "The thief cometh not, but for to steal, and to kill, and to destroy: I am Come that they might have life, and that they might have it more abundantly."

I can see a sparkle from the little stream this morning, where the sun brightly reflects On the water. A sweet fragrance fills the air from nearby Honeysuckle vines. Humming Birds drink greedily, the sugar and water, from the Humming Bird feeder, hanging from the edge of the porch.

Sometimes, I walk down to the shallow water, seeking a little more Solace, from our Creator. Sometimes, I need a special touch from a Higher Power, from somewhere beyond me. PSALM 143:6, "I stretch forth my hands unto thee, as a thirsty land."

A few years ago, we had a drought in our area. I made my way down to the, almost dried up, stream, nearly every day. The neighbor's wells and springs were going dry. Bill and I didn't have the money to have a well drilled. I would remind the Lord, That we didn't have the money, and asked Him, to please keep His hand on the spring.

I didn't see any hundred dollar bills, floating on the water, or hidden in the mud and Rocks, but that pump in the spring, kept on pumping. PRAISE THE LORD! The spring Furnished water for four families at the time. PHILIPPIANS 4:19, "But, my God shall Supply all your need according to His riches in glory by Christ Jesus."

I believe, we all have a, "High Calling," to do. It may not be a song, but I know the Lord, has a plan for all His children.

Don't Let My Song Die In Me

Don't let my song die in me,
Give me the strength to set it free.
Don't let it wither, way down inside,
Before I cross that river deep and wide.

CHORUS:
We all have words, we need to say,
Lord, let them help others, along the way.
If, we're done wrong, help us forgive,
And let out our songs—while we live.

Don't let me block out life, so dear,
Lord, help me embrace what's left here.
Though time is short, it's been long,
Lord, put in me, a brand new song.

Joyce Bennett

I KNOW WHERE YOU ARE

PSALM 67: l, "God be merciful unto us, and bless us, and cause His face to Shine upon us."

I waded through the dew to pick a few blackberries this morning, before the heat set in for the day. I found a few big ones below the old house.

The roof on the back porch has almost fell in. Memories rush to the forefront of my mind. I don't remember much, when Geneva and Virginia lived in the house. It's been a lifetime, since, Bevis marched and sang the Marine Song, with Daddy's shotgun on his shoulder. I also, remember him, nailing some pine logs, high in the air, for us to walk on.

Bevis, moved to Atlanta and stayed awhile with Geneva, and her husband, John, and their two small sons, Micheal and David. It was during this time, he came after Momma, Barbara, and me, to go there for a short visit.

Bevis had bought a car from somebody. I could see the road through the floor, but it must have run all right, because, we passed every car and truck on the road.

PSALM 91:11, For He shall give His angels charge over thee, to keep thee in all thy ways."

I don't remember, which came first with Bevis, whether, it was Peggy then the Marines, or the Marines, then Peggy. It both worked out fine. They have three children, Kenny, Connie, and Keith, and six grandchildren. Bevis, also, preaches the gospel.

Barbara still reigns clear in my mind. There's something about a little sibling, that brings excitement, from just being around them. There's the sweet smiles when their happy, and the frowns, when their not. It was a pleasure to have a little sister most of the time, yet, there were times, when she was like one of the blackberry briars, buried deep, in my heel.

Ellen came over one Sunday afternoon. Barbara, Ellen, and me, walked to a little place we called, "Holly Springs." It was some holly bushes, and it was wet.

We explored some on our walk. We found a bridge over a small stream. Someone had wedged a large jug of whiskey under the bridge. The three of us, wrestled the jug out, but couldn't get it back in place. I soon grew weary and kicked the jug, causing it to roll down the bank into the water.

The Briar-in-the-heel, blackmailed me for days. I had to answer to her, every beck and call, or she would tell daddy, about me rolling the whiskey in the branch.

ROMANS 3:23, "For all have sinned, and come short of the glory of God."

I Know Where You Are

I was mediating one morning, as I often do,
When I heard a voice saying, I am there with you.
Just lean on me, I know every life's scar,
I know all about you, I know where you are.
CHORUS:
I know where you are, for I'm there too,
I am there waiting, to show you what to do.
I own this world, the moon and every star,
I'm in the mist, I know where you are.

My blood was shed on Calvary, but not in vain,
If you would only trust me, and call upon my name.
I am your Savior, I know more than all, by far,
Do not fret, my child, I know where you are.

Joyce Bennett

Bevis and Peggy Southern

Bevis Quay Southern
U.S., Marines Corp.

Barbara Southern Garrett

HE KNOWS EVERY TRAIL FROM MY VALLEY

PSALM 121:5, "The Lord is thy keeper: the Lord is thy shade upon thy right Hand." PSALM 121: 3, "He will not suffer thy foot to be moved: He that keepth thee Will not slumber."

The summer heat has come in full force. I am stiff and achy this morning. I have been diagnosed with Polymyalga. This is pain in your arms, neck and shoulders. There Were times, when I hurt in my lower back, down into my feet, but Thank the Lord, this is some better.

JEREMIAH 30:17, "For I will restore health unto thee, and I will heal thee of thy Wounds. I heard someone say, when you are managing, that is not a healing. I was Prayed for at the church, so many times, I thought about the man that was suppose to Have been baptized so many times, the Tadpoles, knew him by name.

My doctor sent me to a Neurologist, a short time ago. My feet and legs were Hurting. The lady Neurologist, scheduled me for one of the tests, where, They stick Needles in your arms and legs. While she was in the middle of the test, she bent down to my face and said, "We both know what this is all about, don't we?"

I wished I had said. "No, why don't you tell me?"

I went back to the Neurologist in a couple of weeks. She said, "You don't have any Pinched nerves." I was put on medicine for pinched nerves any way.

I'm a member of a Prayer group. We were planning a large Yard-Sale to help our gas fund. My friend, Sue, had several items to donate. I told her, I would come for a visit, and we could put the items in my car.

The new medicine made me nervous, but I didn't think much about it. I was on a Road I hadn't been on before. I was going sixty miles an hour, when I felt a presence in the car. It was a presence that felt like Bill. I immediately, knew it was a warning.

I slowed down, there was a curve, and then I drove under a bridge. Bill's presence was still in the car. I asked, "Lord, can I see him." I didn't hear anything, then I asked, "Lord, can I touch him?" A still, gentle voice spoke to my heart and said, "You don't need to." The presence left. The Lord knew, and I knew, I was healed enough to go on.

I went to a Chiropractor. I told him what the Neurologist had said. He replied, "I don't know what the trouble is, you either have a pinched nerve or you don't, but You do." He asked if I could come to see him three days a week. He was located in a nearby town. I could only go once a week.

When I hurt my back at the store, a hot pain ran down my right leg to my knee. I had Arthritis. I knew what that felt like. I also have osteoporosis, but this was a hot, burning Pain in my lower back. I reported the accident, but thought it would soon go a way. I fell several years before, where I worked. I was stove up a few days, but soon healed.

When I climbed a ladder, I felt like I was going backwards. My balance was off. When I kneeled to put out stock on a lower shelf, it would make me dizzy. When I went to the Bathroom, my kidneys would act, before I could get there. I felt, as if, the veins in my legs were little railroad tracks, with little railroad cars racing up and down them.

Someone, in the office, made me an appointment with a Workers Compensation Doctor.

The doctor did write me an excuse to stay off the ladder for awhile and gave me a high Powered shot. The shot helped my back, but it wasn't long, before I begin to hurt all Over. I was sent for some tests, but every where I went, I felt like they thought I was Trying to get something for nothing.

John, my stepson, asked me to go to his doctor in Atlanta. I went and took the Film From a CT scan and a couple more X-Rays. The doctor told me, I had two discs that were bulged, instead of one. I had two spurs in my neck. The Workers Comp. Doctor, had told me, that there wasn't anything wrong with my neck but, stress. I also had a mild Case of Corporal Tunnel Syndrome. The Workers Comp. Doctor, had told me, it was Arthritis.

I went back to the workers comp. doctor, one more time. I talked to a lawyer. He sent a letter to the store, which did more harm then good.

I worked two years after my accident. I left the place crying. The last work schedule I saw, was four hours each afternoon and eight hours on Saturday. I was going to have to Work six days to make twenty-eight hours. Bill was getting sick and I had reached the Point, I wasn't able to work.

I went a few times to John's doctor, but had trouble getting to Atlanta, and didn't have The money to pay him.

I received a small settlement and was able to draw my disability. MARK 13:11, "But, when they lead you, and deliver you up, take no thought before hand what ye shall speak, neither do ye premeditate: but whatever shall be given you in that hour, for it is not thee that speak, but the Holy Ghost. PRAISE HIS WONDERFUL NAME!

We sometimes have trials, which shake us to the core. This one, was one for me, and is still on my Medical Records against me. But, through it all, I found the Lord, looks at all the picture. Bill became worse and had to go on Kidney Dialysis. I was home to take care of him. I was able to take care of him from the last part of 1997 to the first part of 2004. Bill, spent the last year, he lived, in our local nursing home. I was so blessed to be able to stay with him a lot there.

The Lord knows our future, and I'm so glad, I know Him.

He Knows Every Trail From My Valley

I wonder along, in this dismal shadowed land,
My Lord, knows the path, I must take.
He leads me gently, to be still and wait,
For, He's with me and a new dawn will break.

CHORUS:
Yes, He knows every trail from my valley,
He knows the right one for me.
He sees every rock, each briar in the trails,
And, He will lead me for He never fails.

I need to cross the valley, to reach the mountaintop,
I had to cross that cross, for my crown.
I'm looking for the sunset—just ahead,
And from the distance, I hear a trumpet sound.

Joyce Bennett

Rex and Joyce

Rex

MOVE UP THE MOUNTAIN

JOHN 14:28, "Peace I leave with you, my peace I give unto you: Not as the world giveth, give I unto you. Let not your heart be troubled, neither let it be afraid."

The greenery is so clean and fresh this morning. Early morning sunlight shines In the yard, but yet, to reach the porch.

A storm blew up yesterday evening, leaving a lot of bare limbs in its wake. Trees Bent double, scattering leaves in all directions. Angry, black clouds filled the sky. I Went to the yard, but couldn't see a funnel cloud. I was frightened for a few minutes, But when, I asked the Lord, to keep everyone safe, I began to feel His Wonderful peace, Settle in and around me.

Some tree branches fell in the yard, but not any large ones. Two plastic chairs sit at The edge of the yard, unharmed. Isn't that just like Jesus? Through all the raging wind, Two plastic chairs didn't turn over. PRAISE HIS WONDERFUL NAME!!

I believe the Lord was showing me, if He, could keep two plastic chairs through the Storm, He could surely keep me.

ISAIAH43:2, "When thou passest through the waters, I will be with thee; and through the rivers, they shall not overflow thee: When thou walkest through the fire, thou shalt Not be burned; neither shall the flame kindle upon thee."

Move Up The Mountain

We live so far beneath, God's great promises,
While we fail to believe His Holy Word.
Staying in the lowlands and valleys of defeat,
Instead of on the mountain with the Lord.

CHORUS:
Don't homestead in the valley, move up the mountain,
Jesus waits on you and me,
Come up from the shadows, to the top of the mountain,
Jesus, will bring you sweet victory.

The only true victory is found in Jesus,
We can walk by still waters with Him.
Let your faith wing up, the highest mountain,
The valley cares will then grow dim.

Joyce Bennett

I LOVE YOU, MY JESUS

1PETER 5:7, "Casting all your care upon Him: for He careth for you."

I didn't go out on the porch this morning. I slept a little later than usual. My mind Seems to be filled with indecision.

A few weeks ago, I went by to see, Momma's, half sister, Lillie and her husband, Dock. They lived at the time, in a government apartment, but have since, moved.

I drove down the hill, and noticed the apartments had a peaceful look. The yards were Neatly mowed. I didn't see any clutter in the yards or on the porches. The people in Charge, sure did a great job keeping the place looking good. I believe the seed was Planted that day, for me to ask about an apartment.

I came home and prayed, "Lord, if I can have one of those apartments, before I need To have the gas tank filled, I want to take it, if it is your will." I paid all year for the Winter Gas. When, I finally would get the bill paid, it was time to order again.

There is another reason, in the back of my mind. When night time rolls around, I am Afraid. Sue and Rebekah lived awhile with me, but moved, due to Sue's job cutting Hours. Sue thought she could find a better job in a larger town. Bill is gone, Momma Is gone, and also, Geneva. Sometimes, I feel like a setting Duck, on this hill.

The enemy, of my soul, may be trying to defeat me, but this, also, may be God's Will for my life.

I am so blessed to know, my Lord and Savior, Jesus Christ. GALATIONS 5:16, "This I say then, walk in the Spirit, and ye shall not fulfil the lust of the flesh." I do Not continually stay, in that place in the Cleft of the Rock, but I know it is always there.

One night, as I prepared for bed, I became aware of a presence near me. "Lord, There's somebody here," I said. I then saw a form of a man, about the size, Bill had been. The man was wearing overalls. Bill liked to wear overalls. I said again, "Lord, Someone is here." There was a noise at the door, sounding like someone was trying To knock the front door down with a two-by-four.

I called 911. Some deputies came, but didn't find anything.

Recently, I heard a preacher telling about the Lord, sending an angel in the image of His mother. He said, the reason, The Lord, sent a presence looking like someone we Know, is to keep us from being afraid. This was the second time, this has happened to Me. I know the Lord, is the same yesterday, today, and forever.

HEBREWS 13:8, "Jesus Christ, is the same yesterday, and today, and forever."

I Love You, My Jesus

CHORUS:
I Love you, my Jesus, I do, I do,
I Love you, my Jesus, I do, I do.
I wake up in the morning, to spend the day with you,
I Love you, my Jesus, I do.

There's a mist in the garden, bidding me to come out,
There's peace and joy waiting, if I will never doubt.
The birds are all singing, oh, what a heavenly choir,
I'm going to the garden to meet, my Jesus, there.

The dew is now lifting; I see a sun-ray,
I must move on, oh, how I'd like to stay.
Jesus, go with me, And I'll make it all right,
Stay with me today, and stay with me tonight.

Joyce Bennett

THERE'S COOL WATER IN THE VALLEY

PSALM 104:24, "O Lord, how manifold are thy works! In wisdom hast thou made Them all: the earth is full of thy riches."

How wonderful it is to come out on the porch and feel, The Lord's presence, to hear Scripture filling my mind. To see the morning sun filter through the trees. I saw the old House, one time, wrapped in sun-rays. In the bend of the road, down from the mailbox, is the most majestic place to see sun-rays.

There is nothing in this world compared to the presence of The Lord.

LUKE 10:24, "For I tell you, that many prophets and kings have desired to see those Things which ye see, and to hear things which ye hear, and have not heard them."

I was going to a Deposition, one time. I had asked everyone at the church to pray for Me, but, I needed something more. I could feel a deep hunger in my spirit. A small Gentle voice spoke to my spirit and said, "You will come forth as shining gold." That Was It! I needed a word from my Lord.

JOB 23:10, "But He knoweth the way that I take. When He hath tried me, I shall come forth as gold."

I thank The Lord, for His visitation this morning.

There's Cool Water In The Valley

Dear Lord, you are clothed in greatest honor,
Your robe is wove in majesty.
You stretched the heavens like a curtain,
And you bought Salvation for me.

CHORUS:
You send the springs in the valley,
You water the green hills from above.
You fill the streams and the rivers,
And, You've filled my heart, with your love.

Thank-you, Lord, for springs in the valley,
Thank-you, for the waters cool and still,
And the mist hovering the mountains,
And, Thank-you, Lord, for showing me your will.

The birds sway lightly the branches,
The eagle rises with the wind,
I face life's storm, I see coming,
For on you, My Lord, —I depend.

Joyce Bennett

MY GUEST OF HONOR

Revelation 1:18, "I am He that liveth, and was dead; and behold, I am alive forevermore, Amen; and have the keys of hell and of death."

This scripture came to me this morning. I hear it a lot in my Spirit. I believe, the Lord, is saying to me, "I have all power. I have the keys to hell and death."

MATTHEW16:19, "And I will give unto thee the keys of the Kingdom of heaven: And whatsoever thou shalt bind on earth shall be bound in heaven: and whatsoever thou shall loose on earth shall be loosed in heaven." He also, has the keys to the kingdom of Heaven.

I know, we all are not alike. Some things has happened to nearly everyone, they can Not explain. I am so blessed to have had the mystifications, He has shown me.

One morning, I was sitting in my chair at five o'clock. My soul was burdened, and I was crying out to The Lord, when I felt someone standing beside my chair. It was, My friend, Sister Dottie, in Florida, comforting me, and telling me everything was going To be all right. I could see her mouth moving, as she spoke.

I waited until, I thought, Sister Dottie, had time to be out of the bed, then, I called her.

"Sister Dottie, "I said, when she answered the phone. "You were here with me this Morning."

"Oh, Sister, Joyce," She answered, "The Lord, woke me up at four, this morning, and told me to pray for you . . ." It came to both of us at the same time. Florida time is an hour behind Georgia time. We were both praying at the same time. PRAISE THE LORD!

I have felt the presence, a couple of times, of an old Saint, comforting me when I was sick. The Lord can do anything.

I have had trouble this week, with my stomach. Everything, I eat has been going Through me. I know, I need to eat some cream potatoes, or some oatmeal. I'm craving A Chili Dog. I'm thinking, it's the same crime to steal a horse, as it is a sheep. The food Will probably go through me anyway. I'm going for the horse. I am going to fix me a Chili Dog.

PSALM 145:3, Great is the Lord, and greatly to be praised; and His greatness is Unsearchable.

My Guest Of Honor

I sit down in my old chair,
And reach, for the Bible of mine.
I read in His precious word,
For, this is my best time.
I talk to, my Savior; I'm as peaceful as can be,
And, my guest of honor, honors me.

CHORUS:
Oh, my guest of honor, honors me,
When His presence, comes in and sets me free.
He's worthy of all praise—I'm as honored, as can be,
When my guest of honor, honors me.

Oh, I have had my sick times,
I've seen some sorrow too.
There have been drear—y days,
I didn't know what to do,
But, through, my Lord and Savior, I have victory,
And, my guest of honor honors me.

I went to church last Sunday,
I found His presence there.
I felt Him in the singing,
In the sermon and the prayer.
We worshiped, our Lord and Savior, the one, we all trust,
And, our guest of honor, honored us.

Joyce Bennett

I WANT TO HIT GOLDEN STREETS RUNNING

ECCLESIASTES 9: 11, "I returned, and saw under the sun, that the race is not swift, Nor the battle to the strong, neither yet bread to the wise, nor yet favor to men of skill; but time and chance happeneth to them all." This seems to be life; we go awhile, Seemingly on the mountain, but we all have our share of valley time. I heard an old Lady say one time, "It's not a nickel's worth of difference, between the women who stayed at home and the women who went."

Naomi, the manager, at the Housing Authority, has called me. She told me, a lady Would be moving by the first of the month, and I could have the apartment, if I wanted it. Praise The Lord; I am going to be able to get the apartment.

Memories flood my mind. This has been, Bill's, and my home for years. He loved the porch. This is where, I did most of my crying, when he went on to be with the Lord.

John, and his friend, Sherry, are making plans to help me move.

John, and someone he knew, and his wife Jo, moved us back from Florida. Bill, had Taken sick. It looked like, we were going to loose him then. He stayed a short time in Kennestone Hospital, in Marietta, Georgia. We stayed two weeks with John and Jo, and their two children, Jody and Misty.

John was able to find us a secondhand, singlewide, mobile home. He moved it here On the home place. I gave John an acre and a half, of the five acres, I had inherited from Daddy and Momma. I hoped the land would help some.

When I began, to draw my disability, John found us a secondhand, doublewide. We Had the money to pay for our home, but wasn't enough to pay for all the help. Family And friends, joined in and worked for days anyway. The Lord always makes a way. He Always has a people that are willing.

Time and chance happens to us all. The place by the baninister is empty. The trail to Momma's has grown up. John is now divorced. The bean patch, and Bill's garden has grown up with briars and weeds.

The Lord, reminds me of this scripture.

PHILIPPIANS 3:13-14, "Brethren, I count not myself to have apprehended: but this One thing I do, forgetting those things that are behind, and reaching forth unto those things which are before."(14) "I press toward the mark for the prize of the high calling of God in Christ Jesus." Some precious memories will remain, as long as it is His will, but, by His grace, I can press on.

I Want To Hit Golden Streets Running

I've been through life's tunnel so dark,
I would grasp at just a spark.
I've met people in this world, evil and cunning,
But, it's not, what I've been through, it is where, I'm going to,
I want to hit those golden streets, running.

CHORUS:
I want to hit streets of gold, running, running,
In that land, there so bright and stunning;
Where God prepared a place, built by Mercy and His Grace,
I want to hit those streets of gold, running, running.

I use to swing on the old oak tree,
We had fun, my siblings and me.
I never saw old age and illness coming,
But, once I found the way, to the land of perfect day,
Now, I want to hit the streets of gold running, running.

Joyce Bennett

COME ON SUNDOWN

1CORINTHIANS 2:9, "But as it is written, Eye hath not seen, nor ear heard, neither have entered into the heart of man, the things which God hath prepared for them that love Him."

Echoes from the past, seem to grow even louder, since, I know, I am going to move.

I remember hearing, Bill, call to me, late one evening, when, I was leaving the Nursing Home. I had already kissed him, goodnight.

"Goodnight, Sweetheart," he called.

I yelled back. "Goodnight, Honey."

"By, "he called.

"See you, tomorrow."

"O.K." he answered.

I know everyone, in hearing distance, was glad for our, goodnight, to be through.

I hated for Bill, to have to stay there, but he, required some lifting. It hurt my back to assist him getting up and down.

One evening, when Bill was still at home, I told him, I was going to see about Momma. I had cooked, so I dipped out some food to take to her.

Bill, was never overjoyed, with me, going to see Momma.

"I wish somebody, would put that old woman in a Nursing Home," he mumbled.

I went down the trail, going to visit, my momma, for a few minutes. I hardly, entered through the door, before Momma said, "I wish them kids would put Bill in the Nursing Home."

It was probably funny, hearing this from both of them in one day. I was more bewildered than amused. I didn't tell either one of them, what the other said, for a long time. They were having a feud, and I was in the middle of it.

Sometime, a little later, Bill had a sick spell and did go there. I know, I looked Tired. I had been dying my hair some, but it blended into the gray, so it wasn't that Noticeable. I thought, my appearance needed a lift, so I bought a more daring Hair Color. This time, my hair resembled yellow broom straw. I remember, when I bought the hair dye, I was trying to hurry and get back to Bill.

Well, there I set, with my husband, in a place, he did not want to be, and I had turned from a gray head to a bright blonde. I felt like everyone who saw me, figured, my next Stop would be the nearest Jute Joint.

Life has been hard at times, but it's also, been good. I blink my eyes and look across to my hollow. A cool breeze, gently, moves the surrounding underbrush, outside the yard. A Dirt Dobber, sings loudly, as it builds its dirt home. The Sunshine, has almost reached the swing. I must stop reminiscing and get to work.

ISAIAH 40:41, "It is He that sitteth upon the circle of the earth, and the inhabitants thereof are as grasshoppers; that stretcheth out the heavens as a curtain, and spreadeth them out as a tent to dwell in:"

Come On Sundown

CHORUS:
Come on, Sundown, come on, come on,
Come on, Sundown, come on,
Too many people are sad and alone,
Come on Sundown, Come on.

There is unrest, all over this land,
Come on, Sundown, come on.
Some have forgotten, you understand,
Come on, Sundown, Come on.

I do not worry, about this world's trend,
Come on, Sundown, Come on.
Lord, I only need you, as my best friend,
Come on, Sundown, Come on.

Lord, some have now, turned away,
Come on, Sundown, Come on.
I'm looking for you, just any day,
Come on, Sundown, Come on.

Joyce Bennett

GOD ALLOWED NAILS TO FIX EVERYTHING

PSALM 30:5, "For his anger endureth but a moment; in his favor is life: Weeping may endure for a night, but joy cometh in the morning."

I'm having a quick cup of coffee, before, John and Sherry comes to help me do some packing.

Memories, are even, more real, with the moving drawing near. Most of my memories are so dear, but there are some that hurt. I am going to bring this one up, and hope that the Holy Ghost, will blow it, and any more like it, away, to never be remembered any more.

One Christmas, I called, Odessa, my friend, in England, to wish her, A Merry Christmas. Odessa, had been so sweet, about recording my songs on Cassette Tapes. She still did them, from time to time, even after, she moved to England.

Well, Odessa, didn't want to hurry as fast as I did. We talked a little longer, than I intended.

When I hung up the phone, I said, "I hope that call didn't cost us two hundred dollars.

Bill, and some of the family were sitting there. Bill, didn't say anything.

A few weeks later, I went with a friend, to church. "How much did it cost to call your friend in England? "She asked.

I wondered why, she asked me a question like that. "Eighteen dollars," I answered, "Why?"

"I heard it cost two hundred dollars," She replied.

It hurt me so bad, that someone would lie about me. It had been all around the community, then into another community, that I had wasted two hundred dollars on one phone call. I couldn't remember hurting anyone bad enough, to make them want to hurt me.

TITUS 3: 3-4, "For we ourselves also were sometime foolish, disobedient, deceived, serving divers lusts and pleasures, living in malice and envy, hateful, and hating one another." (4) "But after that the kindness and love of God our Savior toward man appeared:"

We are not skipping through life, without setbacks, but when I think of all the good, that has happened, it over rides, anything else, a Country mile.

Bill's sister, Opal Woodall, and her husband, Charles, were so good to bring us things, And help us, during Bill's illness. His brother, Henry, and his wife, Myrick, came some, also, Our friends, W.H. and Sue Wright, came a lot and set with us on Sunday afternoons.

Clara Bennett, Bill's mother, was so sweet and funny. She was in her nineties, when she called me, one day and said, "Two of the girls are coming, I don't know which two, We're going some where. I don't know where, but we're going." She was laughing. I never seen her, ever, having a bad day.

I belong to the Sweetest church in the world. Pastor Earnest and Betty Allred, with the greatest members ever. I have so many friends. I won't attempt to name any of them.

I remember one time, Faye, a friend, came and brought someone with her to pray for Bill. He had a bad sore on his leg, at the time. Well, Faye, had heard Bill, yelling for me to get off the phone. She was mad at Bill. Well, this prayer Warrier, whom, had been in dozens of homes, to pray for people, had to repent herself, before she could pray at all.

We were so blessed to have, Doctor, David Dennard, He was, Bill's doctor, than later became mine. He makes it a point to know all his patients. I have never been to see him, when he hasn't asked me, "Have you written any more songs?" I still see him every six months. His nurse Marie, than later, Tammy, have also, been great.

PSALM 68:19, "Blessed be the Lord, who daily loadeth us with benefits, even the God of our salvation."

God Allowed Nails To Fix Everything

Jesus, My Savior, was accustomed to nails,
For that had been, His earthly father's trade.
As He, labored day by day, did He know along the way?
Nails would be used, for this world to be saved.

CHORUS:
God allowed nails to fix everything,
Chilling echoes from Calvary, from the hammer's ring,
While Christ, My Savior, suffered the pain,
Yes God, allowed nails to fix everything.

Jesus, was held on the cross by three nails,
They became drenched, with His blood stains.
Through His, intense pain, redemption was gained,
Yes, God allowed nails to fix everything.

Joyce Bennett

David T. Dennard, M.D.
Nephrology & Hypertension Specialists

LET'S GO TO THE OTHER SIDE

1THESSALONIANS 5:18, "In everything give thanks: for this is the will of God in Christ Jesus, Concerning you."

We packed a lot yesterday afternoon. I am waiting to start with John and Sherry. Sherry is the Supervisor. I'm more than willing to let her be.

I have reminisced this morning, back to the time I met Bill. I met him through, his Daughter, Brenda. We were working together at the time.

"Will you have dinner, sometime, with my daddy?" Brenda asked.

"Sure," I replied.

Bill called me. I, immediately, liked his voice. We were going out on Friday night. He came over, one evening, before Friday. "I just wanted to come ahead and meet you." He said.

It was love at first sight for me. Well, not at first sight, for I had seen him, one time, When I stopped at the Hospital to see his wife, Bonnie. I saw him later at the funeral home when she passed a way.

We hit it off real well. He soon asked me to marry him. I thought it was too soon, But, he told me, his children were having nightmares. I already knew, I loved him, so I Agreed.

I was in a large department store, one day, before I met Bill. I saw a light, blue suit. I felt an urgency to put the suit on lay-a-way. I had told Bill, about the suit. He knew The place, where, I had the suit on lay-a-way. He came to my job, one day, with the Suit in a bag.

Wedding Bells were about to ring.

The day of our wedding, someone said, Brenda was observing us, and said, "I just Meant for them to eat together."

Lee was ten, at the time. His name was Leland, but Bill called him, Lee. The first Thing, I noticed, was his little heart would beat so hard, when I hugged him, goodnight. Rex had been fifteen, when I lost him. That had been over two years ago. I hadn't been Around a ten-year-old for awhile.

I knew Lee, was lost without his mother, but I didn't know what to do. We begin to Play, "Brat Girl," at night. I would walk up to his bed, acting real smart, and say. "I let The air out of your Bicycle tires. I busted your Basket ball." The game begin to capture,

Lee's attention. He would sit up in bed to see what this, crazy woman, was going to do Next.

Lee, would pretend, he was telling his daddy, what his bratty sister was doing. I even learned to play more parts. I would pretend, I was Daddy, puffing a pipe. The game Was so much fun. We soon had an audience. Bill and Sue would come in to watch us.

It didn't take long for reality to hit. I felt like the new woman, and everyone wanted the other one. My perspective was upside down, big time. The children wanted their Mother. They had not had time to be over their grieving.

It wasn't long before, Lee wasn't so nervous anymore. He would hide behind a door, When I was passing by, jump out at me, and scream like a Hyena. He would bend over Laughing, and I would grab the wall to hold to.

Sue did babysitting for a friend across the street. She was sixteen and gone a lot.

Robert was eighteen. He had a job and was working.

Brenda and her five-year-old son, Eddy, lived near us.

John and Jo lived up the street with their three-year-old son, Jody. Misty, their Daughter, was born a few months later.

I didn't know my nerves were so bad. I hadn't gotten over Rex, at the time. I know, I tried to make a Rex, out of Lee, but with Lee, that didn't work. I had a dream one Night. I saw Rex, in the dream, walking into a lake, then, I saw Lee walk out.

We rented a house in Gilmer County, close to Daddy and Momma. Lee and Sue moved with us.

Momma and Virginia were so proud. I was finally happy. They didn't know, I was About ready to loose my mind. I didn't know what was happening. I wasn't hurting, so I didn't go to a doctor.

Bill bought two pigs. One of the pigs begins to get sick. I prayed for the pig. It was Sunday. We went back to church that night. I testified about praying for the pig. "That Pig's going to be all right." I declared.

We hurried home after church to check on the pig. The pig was dead as a door-Nail.

It was years later, when I told the congregation, at the church, I attend now, about the Pig dying.

Sister Sherry Clark, stood and said, "Would anybody like for Sister Joyce, to pray for You?"

Nobody moved.

We moved to Panama City, Florida, and lived about eight years. We met a lot of good People. I still keep up with Pastor, Doris Corbin, Sherry Clark, and Dottie Williams.

I remember, Lee and me, use to dance in front of the television, while Bill was trying To watch it.

By the Grace of God, I begin to heal.

Lee joined the Navy. He met Rita, while he was in the Navy, and married. When he Served his time in the Navy and came home, he went to Nursing School. I am proud of Him. He has been a nurse for over twenty years. He's now divorced and has a Beautiful Daughter, Madison.

Sue and Rebekah live near me. They are good to include me in their lives. Sue is divorced and has two married daughters, Selena and Kadi.

Brenda, and her husband, Gene New, live in Templeton, Georgia. They have two Children, Jessica and Sion. Eddy is Brenda's son, from a previous marriage.

Robert never married. He also, lives near me.

John, also, lives near. Jody and Misty, lives here in Gilmer County. Jody is divorced and Misty is married to, Scott Dove.

I am confident; I could call on any of them any time I needed them. I am Blessed, beyond measure.

ISAIAH 60:1, "Arise, shine; for the light is come, and the glory of the Lord is Risen upon thee."

Let's Go To The Other Side

We have heard about the scripture o'er and o'er,
When Jesus said, let's go to distant shore.
They obeyed and sailed across the tide,
For, He said, Let's go to the other side.

CHORUS:
Let's go to the other side,
Let us go, my Savior replied.
He never said, it would be smooth sailing,
He just said; Let's go to the other side.

Jesus, taught by the seashore, on that day,
He fell asleep, as they went across the bay
A turbulent storm arose on the tide,
He rebuked it and they went to the other side.

Do we wait on life's waters to be still?
Are we failing to do the Father's will?
He never said no storms would cross our tide,
He just said; Let's go to the other side.

Joyce Bennett

Bill and Joyce Bennett
August 22, 1975

Leland Edward Bennett
U.S. Navy

Sue Bennett and Rebekah Cruise

Bottom row L-R Sue Bennett and Leland Bennett, middle Brenda New
Second row L-R Robert Bennett, William T. Bennett(Bill), John Bennett

Clara Bennett
My Mother-in-law,
A very special lady

VITORY AT DAYLIGHT

JOB 26:14, "Lo, These are parts of his ways: but how little a portion is heard of Him? "But the thunder of his power who can understand?"

It is only a week now, until the first of the month. The lady living in the apartment, Is being moved this week.

The sun is already shining too brightly, to sit in the swing this morning.

Although, John and Sherry have been doing the heavy work, I have ached, this Morning, from the back of my neck, down to my feet.

It is so wonderful to be able to say, "Good Morning, Jesus, "And feel His Presence. PSALM 121:1-2, "I will lift up mine eyes unto the hills, from whence cometh my help." (2) "My help cometh from the Lord, which made heaven and earth." In His Presence, Pain seems to lose its grip.

I have reminisced a lot about memories from the old house. My memories, past that, Is not very clear. We moved from an old house, a short distance down the road, when I Was six-years-old. I do remember the atmosphere in the house, the day, Daddy and some Of the family and neighbors, were taking our Baby Sister, Lois Carol, to be buried. I was Three-years-old. Someone helped me dress in some navy overalls with a jacket to match. I cannot remember the funeral or them leaving with, little Carol. Momma was real sad.

I remembered, Carol's little baby clothes. I would want to look at them. It hurt, Momma to get them for me, but she did it anyway. I remember the paling fence around the garden. The peach tree, with the beautiful pink blossoms and the flat rock at the front door. We stepped on the rock, to go in and out the house. The house had two rooms, with a fireplace in the front room. The Kitchen was built on the back porch, with a cat hole in the door. We couldn't get off the Back porch. It was too high to jump, and there weren't any steps.

We were riding Truck Wagons, one day. The Forrester children, had came over to Play with us. Emma Lou, Geneva and Virginia, were teenagers.

Bevis and Ermel were Probably, about twelve. Edwin, would have been a little younger. I remember taking my Turn riding down the bank. It was lots of fun.

The truck wagon was a plank nailed on two sturdy tree limbs. The wheels were cut From a pine tree.

Ermel and Edwin had to hoe corn. Ermel didn't like it. "One of the patches, Last year, never seen a hoe, unless, it saw it, while we were hoeing the other patch and it Done as good as the other one, did." He said.

Earnest, their Daddy, made them cut wood for their grandparents, George and Louisa Forrester. "Grandpa tries to get that hot heater in his lap, and Grandma, sits in the door, Fanning." I remember hearing Ermel say.

I also, remember, Bevis and Harold Lowman, wrestling. Freeman, Harold's daddy Would referee.

Momma would take, Barbara and me, years later, after we moved, back to the old Yard at the home place to rake leaves to keep the pigs from freezing. She had so much Patience. Barbara and me, would bury each other, then chase each other, while she Raked leaves. One would hold the sack and the other fill it.

Dorothy Jo and Sheila, our friends and cousins, would come and visit us sometimes. We were blessed to have, had such a wonderful childhood.

One time, Dorothy Jo and me, walked the two-by-fours in the loft of the old house.

We held on to the rafters and walked them. The loft was gone, but the two-by-fours were Still there. Barbara and Sheila were too young to climb up and walk them.

Geneva and her husband, Lloyd, and their teenage, daughter, Lisa, moved back, years Later to the old home place. They lived a few years, in a beautiful single-wide mobile Home, and later replaced it with a double-wide. Geneva was a good sister. When she left home, and went to work, she always bought, The ones at home, a nice Christmas present. She enjoyed life, and would laugh at any Thing. Geneva, had her share of heartaches, like everyone else. She had a hard time in Her first marriage. She left it, taking her two fine sons, Micheal and David. Geneva later Married, Lloyd Clark. They seemed to have had a good life together. Lloyd died a few Years before she did.

Geneva was married two years to George Mooney.

We did not know, Geneva, was as sick as she was. She insisted, she takes her turn, Staying with Momma, while Momma was sick. Geneva, lived only a year, after Momma died. She lost her battle with cancer. We all miss her so much.

The first part of PROVERBS10:7, tells us, "The memory of the just is blessed".

Victory At Daylight

God's anger may endure for a moment,
Weeping can last through the night.
I have found life, in His favor,
For, victory will come at daylight.

CHORUS:
Victory at daylight, oh, victory at daylight,
Joy cometh in the morning, now all is right,
Yes, there's victory at daylight,
Yes, there's victory at daylight.

I'll be leaving this old house some morning,
At the close of a des—pairing night.
I'll lay down this old coat of sorrow,
For, victory will come at daylight.

I'll trade this old house for a mansion,
I'm moving where all is made right,
There the Lamb of God will greet me,
For victory will come at daylight.

Joyce Bennett

Geneva Mooney
Our Precious Sister

ARRAYED IN WHITE

PSALM 104:24, "O Lord, how manifold are thy works! In wisdom hast thou made Them all: the earth is full of thy riches."

There's something about waking early and going out on the porch and seeing, God's magnificent creation. The morning sun gently shines, Birds call in flight, And dew glistens like diamonds. Oh, what a Beautiful day, The Lord has given us.

I look across the two empty yards, I remember, my Brother-in-law, Clifford Mcclure, Waiting patiently, in his truck, for Virginia to visit Momma.

Clifford was paralyzed from his waist down, but had a stick, he used to drive. He Would bring Virginia, over to see Momma, anytime she wanted to come over.

They were both young, when a tree fell on Clifford. He was a Timber cutter, and A Logger. Clifford, and his father, Arvil McClure, were cutting timber when a tree fell On him. I've heard, Clifford, had to help his daddy, lift the tree off himself. His spine Was crushed.

Clifford, Virginia, and their three children, Teddy, Sharon, and Eddy (Bucky), were The most courageous family, I ever knew.

Clifford was in Warm Springs for awhile receiving Therapy. When the therapy Was over and their lives settled down, Clifford, still worked anywhere, he could from A wheelchair. He would roll up to the sink and wash dishes. Virginia, and the children, Worked the garden, and fed the hogs. Virginia did the milking. Clifford helped with Freezing and canning food. He would, even. Help hem, Sharon's dresses.

I always thought it was Amazing, how a Timber cutter, could hem a dress for His little girl. He knew, whatever he did, would take that much work off his wife.

Virginia was always loaded down with food, when she came to Momma's. There Was an elderly couple, living in their community, at one time. Virginia would worry About them. Clifford would drive her, and she would put food in their mailbox.

Clifford has been gone for several years. Virginia's health is failing, but her son, Teddy, and his wife, Sherry, live close. Sharon and her husband, Darrell, also live close To her. Virginia, also, has grandchildren and great grandchildren nearby. She truly is Blessed.

11CORINTTHIANS 4:8-9, "We are troubled on every side, yet not distressed; we are Perplexed, but not in despair," (9) "Persecuted, but not forsaken; cast down, but not destroyed."

Arrayed In White

John beheld the saints arrayed in white robes,
Praising God, around the great throne.
These are they, who came through great tribulations,
And now, have made heaven their home.

CHORUS:
Saying, blessing and honor, glory and power,
Wisdom, thanksgiving and might.
Oh, Praising the Savior, before the throne of God,
Praised the saints arrayed in white.

Oh, the robes of the saints are washed in the blood,
That makes them all purest white.
No hunger or thirst, no tear-dimmed eyes,
In heaven, where the lamb is the light.

Joyce Bennett

Sharon Rogers And Virginia McClure

PAPER DOLL YEARS

PSALM 1:1-2, "Behold, how good and how pleasant it is for brethren to dwell in Unity!" (2) "It is like the precious ointment upon the head, that ran down the beard, even Aaron's beard. That went down to the skirts of his garments."

We are almost ready to move. The lady has moved. We are waiting for the apartment To be cleaned. It is almost the appointed time.

The Lord has given me so many precious memories of here, with Bill, and also, my Childhood.

I believe, my favorite, childhood memory, is playing paper dolls with my little sister, Barbara. We would cut them out of an old Sears catalog. Daddy gave us a pasteboard, Four-room Chicken box. It made a great home for our dolls. We would take them to Church in a shoebox lid. The seats were bent catalog pages. We would bend our dolls at The waist to make them sit.

Barbara would count the dolls. "Give me just one womarn." She would say. I believe When she was through with the women, she went on to the men and children.

Barbara never rushed to the bus stop. Sometimes, I would go on without her. One Morning, I went early, wearing my yellow feed sack dress, with the red flowers. I was Stepping up, on the school bus steps, when she appeared. She was wearing the same feed Sack print, carrying her doll. Wouldn't you know it? The doll was dressed in the same Feed sack. I wasn't very happy that morning.

Bevis could out do the announcer, on his favorite Radio program. "A fiery horse with The speed of light, a cloud of dust and a hearty Hi-Yo Silver." Bevis would say this With the Announcer, but a lot louder.

Momma told this incident, for years. We were going, one night, to a Revival Meeting, Momma knew, Daddy had been drinking that evening, but she didn't Think, he had much. When we arrived at the church, we all hurried in, and down the Aisle, hurrying Daddy to a seat, so, no one would know he had been drinking. We Were all doing well, sitting, smiling and nodding, when a lady came down the aisle, looking for a seat. This wasn't the best time, for Daddy to practice his Gentlemanly ways. He must have been the first one to realize, the lady needed a Seat. Momma said, Daddy looked at her, like he was going to a Hanging, and He was the guest of honor, and said, "I'll give her mine." He walked out and gave The lady his seat. We do not know, how well, he walked out, but he did.

Momma could move her mouth, just like Daddy did, when he said, "I'll give Her mine." We would always laugh.

Daddy drink some, but he wasn't mean to us. He seemed to have liked every-One, he met. He was a farmer. He worked some in orchards and sawmills. When He was young; he taught school some, in a one room schoolhouse. Momma was one Of his pupils.

Momma was Ollie Fowler. The Fowlers were the last people to move from Springer Mountain. Momma, was just a little girl, but she could remember the family moving In a wagon, pulled by two Steers. She said, they stopped and waited for a Swarm of Bees to return.

When Momma, was a baby, Grandma Fowler, took her on a train trip to Canton, Georgia, to see relatives. The train wrecked, throwing Momma in the floor. Grandma, Received a bad head injury.

Grandma's injury never healed. She was taken to the Asylum in Milledgeville, Georgia. She died from that terrible Influenza Epidemic in 1918.

Grandpa Fowler married again. He had two more daughters, Lillie and Josie, by his Last wife, Dessie.

Barbara grew up and married, Robert Garrett. Robert's Brother-in-law, Ray Fowler, Was pastor at River Hill church. Barbara and Robert met through, Ray and Margie Fowler. They have two children, Bobby and Missy.

Barbara and her friend, Brenda Clark, have sang, professionally, for at least twenty-five years. They are part of, "The Melody Singers."

1CORINTHIANS 2:9, "But as it is written, Eye hath not seen, nor ear heard, neither have entered into the heart of man, the things which God hath prepared for them that love him."

Paper Doll Years

Daddy ordered some baby chicks; they came in a box you see,
The box was divided into four little rooms, and he gave it to Sister and me.
It made the prettiest little house for our dolls to stay,
The memory, of those precious years, still lingers on today.

CHORUS:
I'd like to go back to the paper doll years,
Where there were no heartaches, no troubles are cares.
There wasn't much money, but it didn't matter then.
I'd like to go back to the paper doll years and live them over again.

We played in rainy weather, but for us it was sunshine,
There weren't any storms in little sister's life or mine.
"Give me just one more woman," little Sis. would say,
She would get most of my dolls by playing this way.

Daddy and Momma, now have gone, and a sister so dear,
There's another sister and brother that are still living here.
We've all grown older, and seen good time and bad,
But, the paper doll years, as I recall, were the best I ever had.

Joyce Bennett

Elford Quay Southern and Ollie Mae Southern
Daddy and Momma

Robert and Barbara Garrett

HE'LL BE COMING THROUGH THE CLOUDS

1CORINTHIANS13:11, "When I was a child, I spake as a child, I thought as a child: But when I became a man, I put away childish things."

We now have everything ready to move, except a few things I am still using. This is Wednesday. We begin moving Friday morning.

I am so thankful, to The Lord, for letting me open the lid to memories long ago. I'm so thankful for all the hopes, the dreams, and the love of a family. The old house will be as, the former house. It will soon be gone into oblivion. If the Lord tarries His Coming, someone may find an old bottle buried in the ground and say, "That came from the old, Elford Southern, place."

The memories, of my life with Bill, are more vivid. Our Creator doesn't make Mistakes. He made a season for everything. I suppose, I am in late autumn and heading toward winter.

I Praise The Lord for the wonderful seasons. There were heartaches, as I watched sick Loved ones suffer, knowing there wasn't anything more I could do, except, what I was doing. It was also, hard to give them up.

I must go back to a very important part of my childhood, one more time. My Uncle Edd and Aunt Ella, played a big role in my childhood. It was so wonderful to go to their house and play with Ellen, my cousin, and friend.

We had wonderful times, playing in the playhouse. Ellen's brothers, Edwin and Everitt, would play church with us. One of the boys would preach. Ellen and me were busy, fanning our dolls with a funeral home fan. We took turns, Shouting. One time, Aunt Ella said, we had scared their neighbor, Aunt Mary Champion.

Ellen and me had dolls, but I remember, part of the time, we would wrap a long Pumpkin, and fan it.

We would give every bird, baby chick, or anything else, we could find a funeral. One time, we buried a snake. We would sing and hunt flowers for the graves.

When Ellen, was about eleven the twins came along. Aunt Ella, named them, Euel, and Ermel. It wasn't long after the twins, when Ruel, was born. Well, needless to say, We had real babies to hold.

Ellen says, she does not remember this incident. I'm wondering if she doesn't have Selective Memory. We went to a Homecoming, some where, but, I can't remember which church. Ellen and me, had a baby in our arms and headed for the Amen corner. We were pretty young, and soon grew tired, acting like grownups. The house was full, and we were wondering, how we were going to go outside. The twins were being good. We wasn't getting any help from them. I don't know, which one, decided to pinch a twin, or which twin was pinched. (I hope it was Euel). The twin yelled.

Two, sweet little mothers walked out carrying the babies. Some of the people had to move completely, away from the benches, to let us pass.

"They went to a lot of trouble for us." I said, when we made it outside.

"Well, they heard the baby cry." Ellen replied.

Elllen grew up and married Edd Gaddis. Uncle Edd, Aunt Ella, and Edwin, are all Gone on to be with The Lord. Everitt, Ermel, Euel, and Ruel, all married and live here In Gilmer County.

MATTHEW 24:30, "And then shall appear the sign of the Son of man in heaven: and then shall all the tribes of the earth mourn, and they shall see the Son of man coming in the clouds of heaven with Power and Great Glory.

He'll Be Coming Through The Clouds

CHORUS:
He'll be coming through the clouds, when He comes,
He'll be coming through the clouds, when He comes.
He'll be coming through the clouds, He'll be coming through the clouds,
He'll be coming through the clouds when He comes.

We will all go up to meet Him, when He comes,
We will all go up to meet Him, when He comes.
We will all go up to meet Him, we will all go up to meet Him,
We will all go up to meet Him, when He comes.

We will shout Hallelujah, when He comes,
We will shout Hallelujah, when He comes.
We will shout Hallelujah, we will shout Hallelujah,
We will shout Hallelujah, when He comes.

We will see our friends and loved ones, when He comes,
We will see our friends and loved ones, when He comes.
We will see our friends and loved ones, we will see our friends and loved ones,
We will see our friends and loved ones, when He comes.

Joyce Bennett
(We sing this in the tune of, "She'll Be Coming Around The Mountain.")

WINDS OF REVIVAL

HABAKKUK: 3:17-18, "Although the fig tree shall not blossom, neither shall fruit be on the vines; the labor of the olive shall fail, and the fields shall yield no meat; the flock shall be cut off from the fold, and there shall be no herd in the stalls:"(18) "Yet I will rejoice in the Lord, I will joy in the God of my salvation."

For a few weeks, I have watched a Rose bush in the front yard, while passing, going To the mail-box. A couple months ago, I thought, it would, surely, die. Beautiful, red Roses hang from the bush this morning. There's more rosebuds, waiting to bloom, with New branches, springing forth, bringing new life.

The Rose bush reminds me of God's people. They weather the storms of life, but Through, the grace and the power of God, they begin to rise again.

One time, in a service, in Florida, a lady stood and said, "Have you ever tried to kill One of those, Palmetto Bugs? You believe, that Sucker, is dead, then all at once, you See an antenna moving."

I'm enclosing an extra song. I think it's appropriate, for long about now. There is a Line, in the song, that says, "I ain't got time to go out on the porch and sit." I don't know What I would have done without this back porch. This song came to me years ago.

Don't Start Digging

Don't start digging, 'cause I ain't dead yet,
I ain't got time to go out on the porch and sit.
I ain't got time to knit and spit,
So, don't start digging, 'cause I ain't dead yet.

I won't stop going, I will not quit,
I can still throw a tantrum fit.
Move on back, 'Cause I can still hit,
And don't start digging, 'cause I aint dead yet.

I don't change much, my ways are set,
I may be confused and I might forget,
But, I'm still here, and I have my grit,
So, don't start digging, Cause I ain't dead yet.

Joyce Bennett

ISAIAH 40:31, "But they that wait upon the Lord, shall renew their strength; they Shall mount up with wings as eagles, they shall run, and not be weary; and they shall walk, and not faint."

We begin moving in the morning. I'm not leaping for joy, but I am thankful to have Found an apartment. The apartment is small enough to be easy to heat in the winter, also, Easy to cool in the summer.

I praise The Lord, for my friends. Bill and me were blessed with, The Deans, from Wewahitchka, Florida, who came to visit us every fall. Carl and Myrtice, still make the Trip from Florida, to visit me. I am so blessed with friends, at Ranger, Myrtle Beach, S.C., Loganville, Ga., Monroe. Ga., and Panama City, Fl. And Dalton, Ga.

I thank God for all of you in Gilmer County.

I have a wonderful church Family. Pastor, Betty Allred, and all the members, make it Such an honor to be part of it. Dean Petty, is the daughter, of Woodrow and Cora Stover, The Founders of the church. Helen Newberry, my neighbor, and friend, also, attends Faith Chapel.

I realize, this has not been an Emerson, or a Browning, but I have written from my Heart.

I want to honor two Special people in our County. I worked one time, with Farrell Starnes, in a Pharmacy in town. She was so kind to everyone, she waited on. She, Always, treated everyone the same. Farrell, and her husband, Roger, owned the Pharmacy before they sold it. Roger has gone on to be with the Lord. Farrell, has Known many heartaches, but still maintains that same sweet spirit.

The other Special person is Billy Bernhardt. Billy can make a Pauper, feel like a King. He, also, treats everyone the same. Billy is an undertaker. Sometimes, he's seen Putting flowers on graves, where the widow or widower, is no longer able to go to The Cemetery. I believe, Billy, will have Awards, a mile long, down those Golden Streets or across the hillside in Glory Land. The others, who work with Billy, are also, Professional, caring people.

I'll say, Good-by, and try not to think too deep tomorrow, as we move. Who knows? I may turn into a Real City Slicker. (Whatever they do.)

Billy Bernhardt

Roger and Farrell Starnes

Winds Of Revival

We know about tornadoes nearly coming to our door,
We know about wars and rumors of more.
Lives are changing; it seems on every hand,
We need winds of Revival, blowing on our land.

CHORUS:
We need winds of revival, oh, Lord, send the wind,
We need a great awakening that only you can send.
We don't want the troubled winds, but calm would be grand,
We need winds of revival, blowing on this land.

Lord, you formed the mountains and created the wind,
You've declared your thoughts unto every man.
Some have built on the rock, but some on sinking sand,
We need winds of revival, blowing on this land.

We need some time of Pentecost, with a mighty rushing wind,
A place for the young and old, all to attend.
Where all accepts their calling and takes a final stand,
We need winds of revival, blowing on this land.

Joyce Bennett

Edwards Brothers Malloy
Thorofare, NJ USA
October 15, 2013